YOUR PET DOG

REVISED EDITION

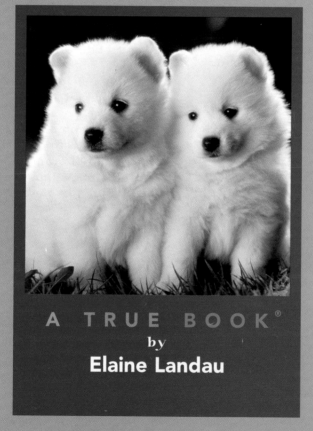

A TRUE BOOK®

by
Elaine Landau

Children's Press®
A Division of Scholastic Inc.

New York Toronto London Auckland Sydney
Mexico City New Delhi Hong Kong
Danbury, Connecticut

A pet dog waiting
for its owner

Content Consultant
Robin Downing, DVM, CVA, DAAPM
Hospital Director, Windsor
Veterinary Clinic
Windsor, Colorado

Reading Consultant
Cecilia Minden-Cupp, PhD
Former Director, Language and
Literacy Program
Harvard Graduate School of
Education

Author's Dedication
For Kait Anne

The photograph on the cover
shows a boy with his border
collie. The photograph on
the title page shows two
spitz puppies.

Library of Congress Cataloging-in-Publication Data
Landau, Elaine.
    Your pet dog / by Elaine Landau. — Rev. ed.
        p. cm. —   (A true book)
    Includes index.
    ISBN-10: 0-531-16767-4 (lib. bdg.)   0-531-15465-3 (pbk.)
    ISBN-13: 978-0-531-16767-0 (lib. bdg.)   978-0-531-15465-6 (pbk.)
    1. Dogs—Juvenile literature. I. Title. II. Series.
SF426.5.L365 2007
636.7'1—dc22

                                                    2006004418

Contents

Owning a dog can be a wonderful experience.

Are You Ready to Own a Dog?

Are you thinking about getting a dog? Dogs are fun and make great pets. It would be hard to find an animal that makes a more loyal friend. But having a dog or puppy also involves a lot of work.

Owners must walk their dogs every day of every season.

Dogs need fresh food and water every day. They have to be taken for walks in all kinds of weather. They should be kept clean.

You will have to take care of all your dog's needs. This means getting your dog help if it is sick or hurt. It also means knowing when your dog needs to rest.

A dog can be your biggest job and your greatest joy. Are you ready to own a dog?

Selecting the Right Dog for You

There isn't one dog that is right for everyone. Different people want different things in a pet.

Some people choose to have a small dog. If you live in a small house or apartment, a small dog might be

This Maltese terrier is small enough to ride in a backpack.

Small dogs are the best choice for many people.

best for you. Small dogs are easier to handle when you travel with them. A small dog also costs less money to feed.

Other people choose to
have a large dog. Large dogs
can be perfect for active
families. They can go jogging
or hiking with you.

Some dogs are large
enough to go hiking with
their owners.

Designer Dogs

A Labradoodle

Breeders are always coming up with new dog breeds. They do this by mating different kinds of dogs. Some purebred mixes are called designer dogs. Poodle purebred mixes are especially popular. Perhaps this is because poodles are very intelligent and don't shed. One such breed is the Labradoodle. That's a Labrador retriever and poodle mix. They get along well with children and other dogs. They are friendly, loyal, and quick to learn.

People who want purebred dogs usually buy them from **breeders**. Breeders are people who mate dogs to produce a specific breed of dogs. They know a lot about their animals.

Ask the breeder about the dog's nature and personality. How is this breed around children? Will a young person be able to handle the dog once the dog is fully grown?

A mixed-breed dog is a mixture of different breeds.

15

Local animal shelters have many pets eager for a home.

These dogs can live longer and are often healthier than purebred dogs.

There are other reasons to pick a mixed-breed dog. While purebred dogs can cost hundreds or even thousands of dollars, mixed breeds do not cost very much.

You can often get a mixed-breed dog for a small fee from your local animal shelter or **humane society**, an organization that works to protect animals. In many cases, you will be saving the dog's life by adopting it.

Do you want a puppy or an older dog? Puppies are cute and cuddly, but they are also hard work. They need a lot of attention. Puppies must be **house-trained**, or taught to relieve themselves outdoors.

If you do decide on a puppy, never bring one home before it is eight weeks old. It is too young to leave its mother before then.

An older dog may not be as cute as a puppy, but it can

This boy is teaching his puppy to relieve itself indoors on newspaper.

still make a wonderful pet. An older dog will probably be house-trained. It may have already gotten some of the shots it needs to stay healthy.

Unlike a puppy, an older dog is often content to be alone.

An older dog also needs less attention than a puppy. Older dogs are happier being by themselves. Is your home empty when you are at school? If so, an older dog may be a good choice for you.

You must also decide whether to get a male or female dog. Some people think females are gentler. Some people think males are more likely to roam. Still others say the dog's breed and nature are its most important qualities.

Taking Home a Healthy Dog

A beagle puppy with clear, bright eyes and a damp nose

Before you take a dog home, check that the animal has:

* a cool, damp nose with no fluid coming from it
* clear, bright eyes
* bright-pink gums
* clean and odor-free ear canals, with no buildup of wax or dirt

A chow chow with a clean, fluffy coat

* a clean, fluffy coat, with no sores or itching
* straight, well-formed legs
* a good nature and personality (Pass up a dog or puppy that is overly fierce or unusually timid.)

Take your new dog to a **veterinarian**, a doctor who cares for animals. Your dog will need a checkup and shots to prevent disease. Bring your pet back to the veterinarian for a checkup every year.

Buying the Basics

You have picked out the dog of your dreams. But before you take home that perfect pooch, be sure you have the basics to care for it. You will need several things:

Bed: Pet stores sell many different types of beds. Pick

Be sure your dog has a comfortable bed.

one that is easy to wash. If you have a puppy, put a piece of your clothing in its bed. Your scent will comfort your new pet during the night.

This feeding bowl has sections for dog food and fresh water.

Food and water bowls: Get sturdy ones that won't tip over or crack. Keep these bowls clean. Make sure to fill your dog's water bowl with fresh water every day.

Food: Ask your veterinarian what to feed your dog. Feed your pet at the same time each day. Puppies usually eat four times a day. Older dogs eat twice a day.

A mixed-breed dog is ready for feeding time.

All dogs need a sturdy leash.

Collar and leash: You'll need these when you walk your dog. Many towns and cities have leash laws. Under these laws, a dog cannot leave your property unless it is on a leash.

Identification information and licensing tags: Make sure to attach proper identification and licensing tags to your dog's collar. If your dog gets lost, it is your best hope of having your pet returned to you.

Your dog will need an identification tag.

Many veterinarians and most animal shelters often implant a tiny microchip under the skin of pets such as dogs and cats. If the pet is ever separated from its owner, scanners can read the animal's identification number and its owner's contact information from the chip.

Brush and comb: All dogs need to be cleaned, or **groomed**. Grooming is important for your pet's health and appearance.

Many dogs enjoy being groomed.

A teething puppy chews on a plastic ball.

Long-haired dogs need to be groomed more often than short-haired ones. Try to brush your dog at least once a week.

Toys: Dogs need their own toys. Toys help dogs exercise and prevent boredom. Your dog or teething puppy needs hard rubber or plastic play toys to chew on. Don't forget that pets with toys are less likely to ruin furniture and other household items!

House-training Your Pet

If you get an older dog, it will probably be house-trained already. But a puppy must learn to relieve itself outdoors. Teaching a puppy to relieve itself outdoors all the time takes a lot of time and energy.

Training your puppy to relieve itself outdoors takes patience.

While it is being house-trained, the puppy should be kept in one area of the house. Put its bed and toys in the same area. The dog will not want to soil its living space.

As soon as you see your puppy sniffing around for a place to relieve itself, take it outside right away. Stay with the animal until it has finished. Be sure to praise your dog every time it relieves itself outdoors.

Reward your puppy for good behavior.

Expect accidents when you house-train your puppy.

Do not expect your puppy to be trained overnight. At times, there will be accidents. When your pet relieves itself indoors, it is your responsibility to clean up after it.

Never scold, shout at, or punish your puppy for accidents. They are part of the learning process.

Don't be frustrated with your puppy if it isn't always obedient.

You and Your Dog

Do you dream of having a well-behaved dog? Then teach it the basics. Consider taking your dog to obedience class so it can learn basic commands such as "stay" or "sit." You will learn the best way to train your pet there.

This dog learns to follow instructions during an obedience class.

You should train your dog not to jump up on people. Your dog may not mean any harm, but it could frighten someone.

Always use praise, not punishment, when training and handling your dog. Praise is an important training tool. Remember that your dog wants to please you most of all.

Be aware of your pet's needs and feelings. A dog is a living creature that depends

A happy dog gives its owner lots of affection.

on you. Your dog will be your best friend. You can be your dog's best friend, too.

To Find Out More

Here are some additional resources to help you learn more about dogs:

 **Books**

Altman, Linda Jacobs. **Big Dogs**. Benchmark Books, 2001.

Berman, Ruth. **My Pet Dog**. Lerner, 2001.

Cole, Lynn. **My Dog: How to Have a Happy, Healthy Pet**. NorthWord Press, 2001.

Foran, Jill. **Caring for Your Dog**. Weigl, 2003.

George, Jean Craighead. **How to Talk to Your Dog**. HarperCollins, 2000.

Jeffrey, Laura S. **Dogs: How to Choose and Care for a Dog**. Enslow, 2004.

Whitehead, Sarah. **Puppy Training for Kids**. Barron's, 2001.

Organizations and Online Sites

American Kennel Club
260 Madison Avenue
New York, NY 10016
212–696–8200
http://www.akc.org/

The American Kennel Club sponsors dog shows, keeps a registry of purebred dogs, and promotes responsible dog ownership. Its site offers dog breed information, listings of local AKC societies, dog-related news, and educational resources.

American Society for the Prevention of Cruelty to Animals (ASPCA)
424 East 92nd Street
New York, NY 10128
212–876–7700
http://www.aspca.org

This organization's site has extensive information on dog care, including tips on grooming, house-training, obedience training, and leash manners.

Dog Owner's Guide
http://www.canismajor.com/dog/

This online publication for dog owners offers details about choosing, raising, training, and caring for the family dog.

Humane Society of the United States
2100 L Street NW
Washington, DC 20037
202–452–1100
http://www.hsus.org/

This organization promotes the protection of all animals. Check out its site for information on pet care, pet adoption, and pet-related news.

Purina
http://www.purina.com/

This site provides information about feeding, grooming, training, and choosing toys for your dog.

45

Important Words

breeders people who mate animals to produce a specific breed

breeds specific types of animal

groom to clean an animal

house-train to teach a dog to relieve itself outdoors

humane society an organization that works to protect animals

mixed-breed dog a dog that is a mixture of different breeds

purebred dog a dog from a long line of dogs that look and act much like one another

veterinarian a doctor who cares for animals

Index

Meet the Author

Award-winning author Elaine Landau worked as a newspaper reporter, an editor, and a youth-services librarian before becoming a full-time writer. She has written more than 250 nonfiction books for young people, including True Books on dinosaurs, animals, countries, and food. Ms. Landau has a bachelor's degree in English and journalism from New York University as well as a master's degree in library and information science. She lives with her husband and son in Miami, Florida.